© HAPPINESS MANTRA
BY SANDEEP RAVIDUTT SHARMA

Table of Contents

Introduction IV

HAPPINESS MANTRA..1

© HAPPINESS MANTRA
BY SANDEEP RAVIDUTT SHARMA

Introduction

This book provides you with a **list of 100 motivational quotes and thoughts** focussing mainly on improving your wellness quotient. Everyone in this world craves to be happy. Instead of wanting to be happy, one should feel happiness within. Most of us assume that by growing rich we may attract happiness. We often fail to understand that money is just a means to satisfy our wants and can never simply buy happiness. Look for happiness in little things of your life and you will find it soon. Just by the sight of beautiful flowers, one can feel happiness without having even a single penny to buy it. When you get what you want, you can feel happiness. If things go the way you want, happiness is felt. This book is just an attempt to present you with motivational quotes which can help you to achieve happiness. I'm sure if you keep reading, referring, sharing these thoughts and quotes, you may derive inspiration and develop a good understanding of various perspectives and facts about life.

"If you are satisfied with whatever you have, you may feel happy. An act of kindness can make one happy.

I sincerely hope, you will find this book amazing, interesting, rejuvenating, unique and constant source of inspiration.

Thank You and Happy Reading.

HAPPINESS MANTRA

© HAPPINESS MANTRA
BY SANDEEP RAVIDUTT SHARMA

Don't assume things in life. Check facts before you comment or judge the other.

God gives us a call to act. It's all up to you to accept and act or reject. Those who do finds the way laid for reaching their destination and enjoy happiness.

© **HAPPINESS MANTRA**
BY SANDEEP RAVIDUTT SHARMA

Appreciate and inspire. When you see someone doing the right thing, do appreciate and encourage them to do better.

Do you like to talk? People prefer those who can walk the talk.

© HAPPINESS MANTRA
BY SANDEEP RAVIDUTT SHARMA

Your timely action can convert your pain into gain. Simply making an action plan will not take you far. Execution with finesse at the right time is the key to success and growth.

© HAPPINESS MANTRA
BY SANDEEP RAVIDUTT SHARMA

You can't force a person to respect you but need to earn it through your selfless attitude and deeds.

© HAPPINESS MANTRA
BY SANDEEP RAVIDUTT SHARMA

Calm mind allows you to load positivity.

Be happy and you can make the world happy. Happiness comes from within. Happy mind has the power to spread joyfulness all around.

© **HAPPINESS MANTRA**
BY SANDEEP RAVIDUTT SHARMA

A good leader never gives up on hope and motivates the team to give their best at all times.

With determination and consistent efforts, the underdogs of yesterday become the King of today.

© **HAPPINESS MANTRA**
BY SANDEEP RAVIDUTT SHARMA

Those who want you to know about their greatness are no great at all.

The drop of kindness from one when delivered multiplies and can become an ocean.

Rescue your thoughts before they decide to go downhill. Good thoughts can lift you up and make you scale the highest peak of life.

Stay motivated always by seeking it whereever you go. Motivated soul can do wonders for this world.

© HAPPINESS MANTRA
BY SANDEEP RAVIDUTT SHARMA

You may want to fly... it's a good thought...to achieve first learn how to stand, walk and run Success cannot be achieved in a day. It's a step by step approach. Have patience and move one step at a time.

The canvas of life is always ready to paint. It's all up to you whether to paint happiness or sorrow.

© HAPPINESS MANTRA
BY SANDEEP RAVIDUTT SHARMA

Those who lay the path to success deserves to walk on this path with Pride. Appreciate their contribution and give due respect.

Innocence reflects in your behaviour and approach towards life.

© **HAPPINESS MANTRA**
BY SANDEEP RAVIDUTT SHARMA

The best thing one can do is keep smiling even when you have lost everything in life.

Be confident but never demonstrate overconfidence.

Break the spell of illusion and accept the ground reality and move forward in life.

You can create your destiny with your own hands, provided you are not holding baggage of the past.

© HAPPINESS MANTRA
BY SANDEEP RAVIDUTT SHARMA

Circumstances force you to act in a given way. No doubt circumstances are not in your control, but you can always control your reaction.

The bond of friendship is stronger than any other relationship. It's all up to you to understand and identify them out of the whole lot who are real or just pretending.

© **HAPPINESS MANTRA**
BY SANDEEP RAVIDUTT SHARMA

Feeling right is better than bright.

© HAPPINESS MANTRA
BY SANDEEP RAVIDUTT SHARMA

© Copyright 2018 Sandeep Ravidutt Sharma - All rights reserved.

In no way is it legal to reproduce, duplicate, or transmit any part of this document in either electronic means or in printed format. Recording of this publication is strictly prohibited and any storage of this document is not allowed unless with written permission from the publisher. All rights reserved. The information provided herein is stated to be truthful and consistent, in that any liability, in terms of inattention or otherwise, by any usage or abuse of any policies, processes, or directions contained within is the solitary and utter responsibility of the recipient reader. Under no circumstances will any legal responsibility or blame be held against the author / publisher for any reparation, damages, or monetary loss due to the information herein, either directly or indirectly. The author own all copyrights.

Legal Notice:
This book is copyright protected. This is only for personal use. You cannot amend, distribute, sell, use, quote or paraphrase any part or the content within this book without the consent of the author or copyright owner. Legal action will be pursued if this is breached.

Disclaimer Notice:
Please note the information contained within this book is for motivational, educational and knowledge sharing purpose only. Every attempt has been made to provide the reader accurate, up to date and reliable complete information. No warranties of any kind are expressed or implied. Readers acknowledge that the author is not engaging in the rendering of legal, financial, medical or professional advice. By reading this document, the reader agrees that under no circumstances the author / publisher is responsible for any losses, direct or indirect, which are incurred as a result of the use of information contained within this document, including, but not limited to, —errors, omissions, or inaccuracies.

If you have further questions, contact on
Tel: +919969256731
Email: sandeepraviduttsharma@gmail.com

© HAPPINESS MANTRA
BY SANDEEP RAVIDUTT SHARMA

Dedication

This book is dedicated to **Goddess Bhairavi**. In the Hindu religion, the Goddess Bhairavi represents divine anger and wrath which is directed towards impurities within us as well as to the negative forces that obstructs our spiritual growth. Bhairavi Mata is also called as **Shubhamkari** and does good things. She is often depicted in images as holding a book, rosary and making abhaya and varada mudra with her hands. She is fiercely protective, lending us wisdom and power, steadiness and clarity. She personifies light and fire, supporting us to reveal what we keep hidden and inviting us to explore our hidden mind and any secret darkness.

I hereby recite the following Bhairavi mool mantra...
"Om Hreem Bhairavi Kalaum Hreem Svaha"
And pray to **Goddess Bhairavi** for lending wisdom and power, steadiness and clarity in the life of my readers and the world. May Goddess Bhairavi protect us from negative forces along with removing impurities of our mind.

© HAPPINESS MANTRA
BY SANDEEP RAVIDUTT SHARMA

Stop when you are not clear about where you want to reach. Give a thought, decide and then move.

© **HAPPINESS MANTRA**
BY SANDEEP RAVIDUTT SHARMA

See the opportunity in challenges and also identify the challenges hiding in an opportunity.

The one who values freedom knows very well that it is not available for free.

It's you who decide what kind of attitude you want to wear today. Make the right choice.

Divine light falls on those who practice kindness, spread message of love and are ready to serve humanity at all times.

© HAPPINESS MANTRA
BY SANDEEP RAVIDUTT SHARMA

You can always work on your limitations with expert advice. Push the performance bar; you have the power to do it.

The hobby of yesterday may become a profession of today. You never know when it becomes the inspiration for tomorrow.

© HAPPINESS MANTRA
BY SANDEEP RAVIDUTT SHARMA

Your perspective decides whether someone is bad or good. We may wrongly judge a person based on whether the view is from a vantage point or low visibility zone.

You feel uncomfortable when you don't get what you want. Condition your mind to remain comfortable and at ease in all kinds of situation.

© HAPPINESS MANTRA
BY SANDEEP RAVIDUTT SHARMA

You may be right in your own way but still, doubts are raised. You either present it rightly or ignore all. Sooner or later the truth will emerge, and it has the power to convince most of them.

Don't give up...try your best...you can still achieve your aim. If needed give up your mistrust, unkind behaviour, arrogance, material pursuit and ill feelings towards others.

© **HAPPINESS MANTRA**
BY SANDEEP RAVIDUTT SHARMA

Attract not only positive thoughts in your life but make full use of them to spread the message of Love, Kindness and Happiness.

Don't shy away if the situation asks you to continue your journey barefoot.

© **HAPPINESS MANTRA**
BY SANDEEP RAVIDUTT SHARMA

Simplicity is the solution to complex problems of the world.

A successful leader is one who could win by optimising efforts, time and energy of his team with a sound strategy for the opponents.

© HAPPINESS MANTRA
BY SANDEEP RAVIDUTT SHARMA

Simple solutions to complex problems, not everyone, can think.

*The smile doesn't cost at all...
Keep Smiling...*

© HAPPINESS MANTRA
BY SANDEEP RAVIDUTT SHARMA

When you are ready to receive, God will shower choicest blessings on you. All you need to do is maintain the purity of your thoughts and deeds.

History is interesting to read, but it would be a matter of pride if one can create history through sheer courage and thoughtfulness.

Don't attempt to test those who love you. In the process, you will lose them.

You can use a mirror to reflect light where it is not reaching, but the same cannot be said about darkness.

© HAPPINESS MANTRA
BY SANDEEP RAVIDUTT SHARMA

Giving excuses over failure is common knowledge but giving due credits to the winner is the hallmark of a future leader.

The world is beautiful forever for those who are looking for good things in life.

The time bomb keeps ticking and exploding at regular intervals. Only those who are too fast and too slow can hear the explosion and face the consequences. Live NOW.

History may not always speak the truth.

© HAPPINESS MANTRA
BY SANDEEP RAVIDUTT SHARMA

Success is just a milestone you have to cross and keep going till you reach the next.

As you wait for your train, there are others who are eager to get down from the halting train. The beginning of your journey can be the destination of the other.

© HAPPINESS MANTRA
BY SANDEEP RAVIDUTT SHARMA

When you failed to change others, why not make one more attempt to change yourself.

If you happened to dial the wrong number, no way you can be in touch with the right person. Same way embarking your life journey in the wrong direction can't take you to your destination.

© **HAPPINESS MANTRA**
BY SANDEEP RAVIDUTT SHARMA

Avoid cursing someone when you don't get the kind of response you expected. You may not be fully aware of the reason why someone didn't respond. Also, it's the choice of the other person to act in a given way.

Self-belief is the first step towards success.

When you are happy, the world seems to be on your side.

You would never know the truth unless and until an attempt is made by you to seek it.

© HAPPINESS MANTRA
BY SANDEEP RAVIDUTT SHARMA

Your dreams define your destiny. Your efforts define your life path. Your passion quickens or delays your success. Your persistence ultimately makes you a winner.

© **HAPPINESS MANTRA**
BY SANDEEP RAVIDUTT SHARMA

Words of wisdom don't help everyone. It helps those who accept them by heart and not just by their ears.

Drum beats cannot silence the voice of truth.

Dare to choose the unexplored path.

© **HAPPINESS MANTRA**
BY SANDEEP RAVIDUTT SHARMA

Improve on your performance each day, and you can touch excellence someday.

© **HAPPINESS MANTRA**
BY SANDEEP RAVIDUTT SHARMA

If you are into business, do enough to know your customer well before your competitor does.

At times your mind makes you think of friendship as love. You may then wrongly blame the other if they leave you. Stay being friends and remove the cap of misunderstanding.

Shed your ego at the earliest. Even the mighty Sun faces a time when darkness engulfs it. Those who don't carry the baggage of ego are sure to rise again after the life-threatening situation.

© HAPPINESS MANTRA
BY SANDEEP RAVIDUTT SHARMA

Never let your ego obstruct your view of the vastness of the world. Shed your ego, and you can see not just the glowing cloud but the sun as well.

Have you thanked anyone today? Expressing gratitude creates positive energy chain which multiplies with every thanks.

If you can't stick to the schedule most of the time then why make it in the first place.

© **HAPPINESS MANTRA**
BY SANDEEP RAVIDUTT SHARMA

Sometimes the pain and sufferings pave the way for reaching out to the biggest gifts of life for you.

© HAPPINESS MANTRA
BY SANDEEP RAVIDUTT SHARMA

It's good to know that you are anxious to face challenges but remember not to go too much into the future. The infinite loop of thoughts for the future can result in an anxiety attack. Anxiety can damage your mental composure and calm to a great extent. Break the chain of thoughts and fear of the future by staying in the present and focusing on what you can do today.

The beautiful mind often forgets the hunter while beautiful heart forgives the hunter. It's better to forgive than forget the ones who tried to harm you.

You decide to make amends in your behaviour. That's the journey towards self-realisation.

Make the most of your life by looking for good things in life.

You are going to make it ultimately only with self-belief.

Rotate your anger, greed and jealousy immediately with understanding, selflessness and friendship.

© HAPPINESS MANTRA
BY SANDEEP RAVIDUTT SHARMA

You may take one step to embrace change. The change will pull you 10 steps in to greet and empower you.

Hit your critics with your win and nothing else.

You are beautiful and amazing. Believe these words.

Friends accompany and may inspire you up to a certain distance. Be ready to complete your journey all alone by remembering the inspiration.

© **HAPPINESS MANTRA**
BY SANDEEP RAVIDUTT SHARMA

The beautiful mind can never imagine a negative world and always craves to build a gentle and kind world.

As you decide to move the mountains, the stones are bound to roll in against you. Face them and you can win.

© HAPPINESS MANTRA
BY SANDEEP RAVIDUTT SHARMA

Your silence can hang an innocent if you happen to be the main witness. Always stand firm in favour of the truth.

Never let success and compliments make you arrogant. Introduce them to humility and continue your stride to achieve more.

Pass on the torch of light to the next generation before we get close to the end of our journey.

© HAPPINESS MANTRA
BY SANDEEP RAVIDUTT SHARMA

Your dreams are not for sale, but it can be shared.

© HAPPINESS MANTRA
BY SANDEEP RAVIDUTT SHARMA

The clock may stop but not the time.

Shed your ego at the feet of the Lord, and your soul is liberated.

© HAPPINESS MANTRA
BY SANDEEP RAVIDUTT SHARMA

Sometimes your ego stops you from appreciating others whenever it is due. You may assume that only you are eligible to do the right and best thing in life.

© HAPPINESS MANTRA
BY SANDEEP RAVIDUTT SHARMA

Those who proclaim that they have a practical understanding of almost everything can be true only to the certain extent as first of all there is no one in this world apart from the almighty God who knows the complete truth. Shed your ego of knowing everything and surrender all your Karma to the Lord and enjoy unlimited bliss.

© HAPPINESS MANTRA
BY SANDEEP RAVIDUTT SHARMA

Change is inevitable. Embrace change with a positive attitude.

Humanity exists due to goodness and kindness holding the forte of life.

© **HAPPINESS MANTRA**
BY SANDEEP RAVIDUTT SHARMA

Not every train can take you to your destination, double check before you board.

The smile is a blessing of the creator given to each of us. Few are reluctant to use it. Keep smiling...

Sometimes doing something is better than doing nothing as it can take you to at least somewhere and not just freeze in your current place.

© HAPPINESS MANTRA
BY SANDEEP RAVIDUTT SHARMA

If the golden Sun can sit down every day. Why can't we put down our ego and live in harmony?

Silence tells a lot if you are paying attention.

Testing times are here to pass. Your knowledge, patience and core values are good enough to meet and greet such times.

© **HAPPINESS MANTRA**
BY SANDEEP RAVIDUTT SHARMA

Start building the road of prosperity from your home of self-belief.

The world around you is changing faster than you can think. Lead the change.

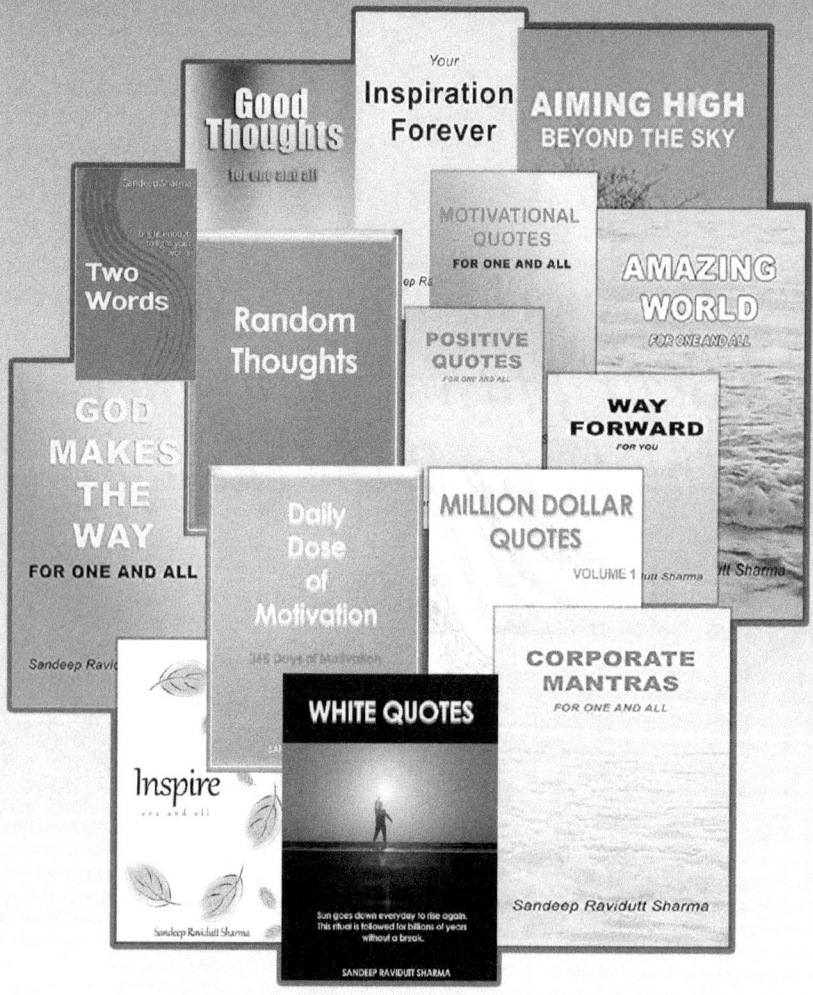

www.ingramcontent.com/pod-product-compliance
Lightning Source LLC
Chambersburg PA
CBHW070803220526
45466CB00002B/524